Jeremy Reed's range and originality as a poet and novelist has been acclaimed by many reviewers, among them J. G. Ballard, Seamus Heaney and David Lodge. He has published many volumes of poetry, notably *Pop Stars* and *Sweet Sister Lyric*, both from Enitharmon, and *Selected Poems* (Penguin), and he has received the Eric Gregory and Somerset Maugham Awards. He has translated the work of Montale (for Bloodaxe), Novalis and Cocteau (for Enitharmon), as well as writing critical studies of Rimbaud, de Sade and Lautréamont. His novels include *Chasing Black Rainbows*, based on the life of Artaud, and *Dorian*, a recreation of the life of Wilde's Dorian Gray. Reed is also a noted writer on pop culture: for Creation Books he has written bestselling studies of Marc Almond, Brian Jones and Scott Walker.

For my Darling Fanchon

Jeremy Reed

Saint Billie

*whose love and support
has allowed to me to
write so many books,
this one dedicate to
you comes with all
of your poeti love*

Jeremy

London
ENITHARMON PRESS
2001

First published in 2001
by the Enitharmon Press
36 St George's Avenue
London N7 0HD

Distributed by Littlehampton Book Services
through Signature Book Representation
2 Little Peter Street
Manchester M15 4PS

Distributed in the USA and Canada
by Dufour Editions Inc.
PO Box 7, Chester Springs
PA 19425, USA

ISBN 1 900564 62 9

British Library Cataloguing-in-Publication Data.
A catalogue record for this book is available
from the British Library

Enitharmon Press gratefully acknowledges
financial assistance from
London Arts and the Arts Council of England

Typeset by Colin Etheridge
and printed in Great Britain by
The Cromwell Press, Wiltshire

❧

For
Fanchon Fröhlich

Contents

STORMY WEATHER

Take me so bluely, greyly, stormily,
and always blackly, inconclusively,
into that bluesy, jazzy song,
it's Lena Horne, or Billie Holiday,
perhaps even Sinatra's rounding out
of love's moody, sad inequalities
I'm playing on this rainy day,

reflecting on old unrequited love
left like a red glove on the beach
for the highest wave to retrieve
and scoop into the frothy swash.
Don't easy couples marry on the beach? –

a black car standing by for a white dress
a black dress standing by for a white car.
Billie could find no equal in a man.

Pre-thunder clarity, and sassy pinks
luminous under density
building as massive cumulus.
Something will break; a sonic riff

bring back the sharpest memories,
the ones that bite like lemon juice.
I play it over, 'Stormy Weather',
the way she gets the rhyme on 'together',
before the vampish hurt breaks through
gritty with memories, and the fast rain
orchestrates every shade of moody blue.

SHOPPING

For a clear space
a blue ceiling
a Patou scent a
new start a cloud
roofing St Moritz
the perfect man
a dream apotheosis
hearts sequins sherbet
liquorice aniseed
a door in the mountain
to my dead mother
foie gras silk lingerie
other people's voices
analogued on record
a place in the desert
invaded by dreams
alhambras remudas
bermuda triangles
polaroids Rolls Royces
a gap between moments
between nanoseconds
stilettos a river
with a gold spine
autumn a château
a red Chanel lipstick
caviar REM
a personal angel
chromosomes opium
red snapper sushi
Sinatra's fedora
and a hole in the sky
for me to climb through
and ask why

ALL OF IT

Why not give all of it. A creative talent as a life, not as the compromised facet of a talent. My voice couldn't come from anywhere else, but an index of biological awareness. The sensitized word I lift into breath, and distil through my phrasing. A Billie-ism. Billie's blues. Why not Billie's whites or Billie's reds. Singing the heart out until there's a hole through it like a scored apple. That way something's always unfolding, like the inexhaustible associations the nerves make, no rendition of a song ever sounding twice the same.

Maybe it's something I've forgotten which my voice is endlessly trying to locate. A face, a dream, a clue, a location, the number on a door, the name of a street, a song, the page of a book, something my mother told me before I was born, or something I'm supposed to know after I'm dead. I fish deep for the unnamed conundrum. And what if I found it, would my voice stop on the moment? Would it just go out, be altered, or cut in half? People who go fishing lose all notion of their possible catch. They cast for fluent ideas teeming across the pond. They wake up with their eyes open on the other side of time. They're in a boat sitting in the middle of a field. Cows are nosing through the clustered daisies, chomping galaxies all afternoon.

Sometimes I debilitate the phrase. I crush analgesics into the note endings. It's like the song is doped with Nembutal. It's always night when I sing. Night on the outside. Standing up like Africa on its hind legs.

I met a man. A crazy man. A druggy man. A nowhere man. He wanted to whip me with a diamond necklace. He wanted to tell me I was the song and not the singer. So I said, 'make love to the words and not me.' And he tried, but he said there was too much sadness to inspire passion. He complained that my numbers were too slow for his rhythm. I became his ideal, and his idol. There was wind all that summer. I remember seeing the trees running like I was watching them from a car. I was standing still and they were moving. Or was I moving and they were standing still? I can't remember. Time is part of death. The highway's always aimed dead true beyond the last town.

BABY PLEASE

Song opens orange curtains in a room
overlooking a very modern world.
Sinatra's voice hits octaves on the air,
fog does a kundalini on the river's spine.

'I have distractedly smashed into things' –
Dinah Washington steps out of her dress
into a raging contretemps
up on five-inch heels in the dressing room,

her pianist flapping in his stripy shirt.
It's faulty intonation stops the heart,
the voice as it confides a hurt
so close it lives as our best friend all day,

the singer talking unrequited love
into a fourth-floor living room.
Dinah calms down, redresses, goes on out,
her tone warms like a cat around the mike . . .

One day she's forty singing in a club
and yet it all seems an extended day,
they talk of Lady and the legend runs
like someone jumped on to a speeding train,

clinging for handholds on the baking roof,
an outback wooden station hurtling by.
Dinah works with the tear along a phrase,
her seventh husband scorching in his seat,

the waitress nudging gossip in his ear.
The singers' lives storm down the century,
their gift travels the airwaves, all of it
amazing, nerve-stripped, hanging on the beat.

Slip Away

The agent parks up in a white Chevy;
thunder lays reverb in the violet sky
building above the airport, grounding flights.
Lady's Cadillac snakes back into town.

A caustic saltiness has furred her voice;
the ladder in her stocking's a zigzag
irritant to her eye. The agent's car
trails like a white shark through the driving rain,

full headlights blazing at the crystal wall.
The pressure's like a fist stood on her nape,
her bite at stardom cracks into her fine
exquisitely attuned naïvety . . .

Once it was easy, cleaning as she sang,
working a mop over a brothel floor,
rehearsing how her life would turn
on an eventless Baltimore pivot . . .

Living on borrowed fame, she can't make right
the continuity. She thinks she's dead.
Yesterday happened a long time ago
like waiting in a forest for a train,

it has that sort of unreality.
Thirty red roses won't keep her alive
but sensitize the woman clued inside
a nerve-shivery vulnerability . . .

Cotton pickers are in her blood. She dreams
of freedom, is it under Southern skies?
a simple cotton dress whipped round her legs
and rain boiling off the edge of the world.

YOU SPIN ME ROUND

Indian summer. The delayed light's gold-dusted on the parked limo. Billie sticks her toes out into the warm air, her head and torso thrown back against the leather upholstery. Her accompanist sits outside rolling a joint. He wears Howard clothes and Tom McAn shoes, his pink socks rolled down. He laughs to himself and keeps on reiterating the word 'motherfucker', like a primordial mantra. Billie's catching sunbeams with her stockinged toes. Red, orange, mauve, yellow, green. It's like October will last for ever. The illusory golden age. Inertial days, and misty nights. Every moment immemorialized by its mellow serenity. There are hot stones in the sky, aerolites which impact with savage indentation. Splinter fallout which dusts the countryside. Little bits of Alpha Centauri exploding across our planet.

Billie curls her toes. There's a red aureole around the sun. She reflects on how you can't ever reverse bad luck. All the scenes, the wrong career moves, the press scandals, the imprudent backstage fights, the narcotic scandals, the switch over from swing to jazz to torchy pop, somehow it's all a part of her and it's not. She has missed most of what has happened to her, like the experiences belonged to someone else. Heroin leads to serious detachment. So too does performing. If she gave herself every night, there'd be nothing left. The chanteuse has never broken through to become a recitalist. She has never succeeded in leaving a nefarious club scene for concert halls. She thinks of the incessant stereotypical pushers. She can teleport these simulacra anywhere. Same eyes that know you know, same demands that meet with equivocatory affirmation. Extortion is a currency proportionate to illicit need. Billie's heard the same coercive terms so often that they're on tape in her mind. Even if the man wasn't there she'd be conceding to a price. She'd be somnolently arranging terms.

They've parked up and they smoke. Billie feels so relaxed she could spread her body right across America. She is without motivation. She wants the Indian summer to last for ever. When she's living out of time she can believe death is a state concerning everyone but herself. She falls asleep. In her dream she's going one way and the car the other.

HEART ON A SLEEVE

An orange deckchair in an autumn park. It fills with orange leaves the colour of October. Someone left a letter behind on the seat, and rain has smudged the ink. It always rains in parks even if the surrounding streets are in bright sunlight. The rain's an act of concentration, like a voice in a club, which is heard only by a few. The rest are hearing themselves, and the interposition of their own internal dialogue. It's like the 500 men who walked across a silent desert, and only one heard the word, felt it enter his bloodstream, and was changed for ever. He remained silent and listened. When he spoke it was to intone the mantra Nam-Myoho-Renge-Kyo. There were extraterrestrials in the desert. Their ship was lit up. They were transmitting back to their star.

Billie walked out to the street and dropped her sunglasses. She jumped back from the impact of light. She had never seen the world this bright or close-up. It was like a stranger. The buildings were blindingly white. It was as though the whole city has just dropped there out of the sky. A delusional mirage, a visual and audial hallucination. Everything was crowding her out by its over-exposure. The photons were an atomistic attack on this frequency. She needed something to hold on to like a song. 'Wherever I put the tune, she found the groove and made it happen. She could swing in the hardest tempo and float on top of it like it was made for her; when I put it slow, she sang it slow – but the most beautiful slow you ever heard.'

Back in the car, behind dark glass, things rectify. She settles back to a world made familiar by its distance. Externals are too menacing for her visual assimilation. She's forgotten the natural identity of things, and lives in a world of signifying ideas about things. She can't remember having seen a tree or a bird or a plant outside her head for years. She trusts that they exist, like air and the blue sky. She wears gloves as a further separation between herself and immediate tactility. And mainlining keeps her even further back. There's a little moment at which she smiles, when the car swerves at a certain point in the avenue. It's like falling downstairs without moving. It's like singing. Giving yourself without ever losing the pain. Her second pair of glasses are dark blue like the sky.

COLD TURKEY

She tents her blue mink on the cement floor.
Eight hours without a shot in the stone cold.
Green icebergs stuck with flags go by the door.

Her pet chihuahua has a lion's head,
it hunts a zebra into a corner
and lays out midget trophies on her bed.

Her silk stockings look like a statistician's
fluctuating graph, they've so many tears.
She counts the ladders with slow precision,

like she is mapping out a secret chart
to reach the angels. They are everywhere.
They dart like speeding swallows round her heart.

Sometimes she thinks she's back in Baltimore
and then the cold turns hot, her arteries
are detonating from a solar core.

The cold returns. She's forgotten her name.
There's no-one there to answer. There's a black
and empty spinning halo. It's called fame.

She searches for clues to identity
like someone wanting something from the snow,
the glare killing off even memory.

She goes on looking. They will bail her out,
delirious inside a white sheet,
and that's what feeling words is all about.

HERE'S LOOKING AT YOU BABE

Autumn in Paris; the bathroom tap swings
in her notation. She is quizzically
childlike about words; they are building blocks
to be licked into shape by breath,
just drop an octave and intonation
means singing all around the song.
She'd like to write, but only stubs a vein.

A foggy blue Ile Saint-Louis.
She thinks she hears Lester Young's saxophone
winning its way through river sounds,
an eerie virtuoso chord sequence
issuing from a sluggish barge. The fog
drapes scarves over an oxidized gargoyle
sat like a pilot at controls
negotiating unscheduled lift-off.

She hangs out in the bar at Le Blue Note,
wrapped up in heady furs.
                              She's right off key
in her impromptu minutes on the stage,
singing, 'I'll Never Smile Again',
a button popping off her dress.
Paris to her means a Givenchy gown
and no money to eat. She leads the way
by giving style to everyone
who bends notes, understates the perfect phrase,
and lives out song. They're playing her today
in cafés here and there, all over town.

You'll Lose Me On a Million Rainy Days

Out West or East or North or South there's this ivy-covered loss in her heart. They're all out there singing in other clubs: Sarah Vaughan, Dinah Washington, Carmen McRae. But none of them have her electricity. The second Billie enters a club, they stop talking. It's like being pricked alert by a needle in your dream. You don't wake up, but consciousness assumes a different tangent, another twist in the disjunctively sequential plot. There's a hanging stair she remembers in a dream. Joe's at the bottom of it sorting through her money and papers, and she can't get down to the level he's on. There's a white piano on that floor, and cage after cage of crazy birds clashing like tropical lightnings with the bars. She fumbles the microphone back in its stand after eight songs. That's her limit now. She can't sustain it longer with or without adjustment. She has always cut free of optimum performance. Something within her fears completion. She'd rather perpetuate the myth of the great failure. The one who falls short like a summer's day abruptly breaking into rain and the pink eyebrow of a transitory rainbow. What is death, she asks herself. Is it the black egg occupying a space by itself in the refrigerator? Is it the gap between her singing and what the audience hear? Is it the interlude between sleep and dream – that blackout into something like the grey, neutral volume inside an airport terminal? She looks for death inside a bunched stocking. And inside the possibilities that there's a sliding compression-door in the sky. Sometimes she sees herself inside her head and she grows terrified. She thinks of this as a close confrontation. She thinks there's no way out of that one.

A million rainy days. Does anyone have that many? It even rains when she's in the cinema watching French films. Or it feels like it could rain in those highly stylized photographs of her taken by Robin Carson and backdropped by Greer Johnson. It's the story of a life, the incremental index of cells dying while the lights are on over Broadway. She sits in the bath for three hours and doesn't know the water's stone-cold. A bath the colour of lapis lazuli. She's improvidently late for the show. It's always later in her mind, for time no longer connects with her chemistry. She lives in an atemporal blank. The car outside her window will meet with the intersection in 2,000 years.

THE CONTINUING STORY

Johnny Square has taken a job selling records in a specialist shop. He has to leave Scarlet behind, and Gina Cube wants to marry one of them, or possibly both. She isn't sure. Scarlet would like to flaunt herself in the shop, and upstage the glamorous photographs of torch icons on record sleeves. He had to imagine Scarlet's iconicity through Billie's. It's the same sense of doubling or duality. Like seeing the wind through a keyhole, and not knowing it's the wind. Scarlet's identityless like the wind, she's more a constant feeling or apprehension to Johnny. Someone creating a storm at his interior. All he knows is that he'd die for her, like he wouldn't for Gina Cube.

Johnny sells Billie's original pressings at bumped up prices. The inflatable evaluation of posthumous fame. Money that never reaches the dead. He keys into Billie by retrieving her vocal fingerprints. Today he sold an original of *Lady in Satin*. A late recording, but still good to have in its original sleeve.

When Johnny takes a break, he buses to the edge of town. He always visits the same place. There's a deserted linesman's hut in a cluster of trees. The train no longer comes through, and giant thistles tear up the rails. Johnny likes to sit inside the hut and attune to ley-lines. He imagines the passengers who once used this line. They were all going somewhere and hoping to arrive. Johnny once found a letter in a rust-coloured biscuit tin in the hut. The note read: 'Meet me on Thursday. I have the key. Love Suzie.' Johnny imagined Suzie wearing a red dress on a Thursday in 1983. Her blonde hair done in a cameo bob. It must have been June – he had decided that. Maybe Suzie was the linesman's piece. Their each clandestine rendezvous marked by a secret note. Johnny sits there, and Scarlet talks into his silences. 'I'm more beautiful than Suzie,' she whispers. 'Your inner dialogue is with the woman who man lacks. You need me to effect the process of your androgynization. I'll be your truest and your only love.'

Johnny listens to that voice in the clearing. If a train came through he'd board it. Suzie would be the only passenger on a train headed South. She'd be wearing a red dress, and her blonde hair would be bobbed. Her skin would smell of crushed silk. They wouldn't talk at all. Suzie would pen a note he'd read later. 'Meet me on Thursday. I have the key. Love Suzie.'

ALL OF ME

The clear hours, how they burn so lucidly,
they're like a bright autumn day in New York,
impacted, windowed, like a white sea-bed
seen through a convex surface. When she gets
the whole of life on speedy overdrive,
she fixes for security,
a downmood stabilization, and pours
gin for her rhinestone-collared chihuahua.
She lies back on the bed, sings 'All of Me',
surprised she knows words she could never learn.

Tonight, a second at Carnegie Hall,
calling the numbers *sotto voce*, split skirt,
white fingerless gloves caught around the thumbs,
seesawing motion of the arms, the head
framed in an agonized posture,
fingers turned in, voice just behind the beat,
she sees herself like that, and blanks the day
inside a hotel room.   When she thinks back,

there's no redemptive childhood, just the space
her voice occupied, and the many loves
described by song, and their bittersweet taste,
a girl from nowhere, nothing, with a way
to read emotion in her heart,
but nervous, using image as a screen,
on stage tonight, bending her toes to roll
a silk stocking along her leg,
rehearsing who she is. And that's her part.

LYRICISTS

Cole Porter sips a Harvey Wallbanger,
thumbing the song-sheets pinned by an ashtray
out on the breezy terrace. Rhyme by rhyme
the epic theme's miniaturized –

a Tolstoy novel got in 40 lines
with such hooky immediacy
the phrasing hangs in on a summer's day
and sticks a lifetime in the listener's mind.

The art talks up inconsequential things
as undercover poetry,
mooded by how a man in purple shoes
read life as melismatic journeyings,

its lesions and sweet cherry on the top.
He tilts a clipped fedora's brim
as fog soaks on the Pacific,
dry-icing with its fluffy lexicon.

A generation defined by its song,
it's more the ambient vocabulary
by which we live, Sinatra bending notes,
invoking midnight as he starts to sing

'Autumn in New York' or 'Foggy Day.'
The lyricist flavours the century,
alerting age to youth again.
He raps out chopstick percussion. His friend

walks naked to the bathroom. Time zips by.
A concentrated sonic feedback roar
builds on the grip of things, the summer day
is blasted to the back of a blue sky.

PEGGY LEE

And when she sings, she leads you into style,
a sort of blued out, median territory,
her phrasing perfect, as she wears
the song like a designer gown,
just so much heart in red tatters, the rest
is note by note par excellence
accomplishment, the blonde who gets it right,
the placement of her black spaghetti straps
as punctuated as the words
she reads transparently. I love that song,

'Fever', and the mood it evokes,
its little story jumping out of a decade
characterized by espresso bars,
bitsy polka dot bikinis,
summers smelling of beaches, and the boys,
the leather bikers dusting up the night.
A Coca Cola bottle blinking in the sky.

She sings across the years as permanence
about the old confusions, love and loss,
the fear of being on your own
on rainy Sundays, nothing but her songs
for consolation, she whose life
went tragic, hear her in the lonely night
affirming that she's nothing but a star.

ONLY THE LONELY

Standing in a silk dress on a dust road
she apprehends the future. It's a car
burning to nowhere with the passenger
scooped from torrential thunder-rain.

Jolting alive into the mirrored bar,
the car a red vanishing point,
it's loneliness comes back at her, despair
that love has never come to stay
that love has walked all over her in boots
that love dematerializes by day
and returns with a wounded foot by night.
That love is everything she'll never have,
no matter she runs out into the street
arms open wide, naked beneath her fur.

Sharp suit, bright tie, the man beside her deals
and it's her husband. She is burnt by pain
and dreams she'll find the car outside,
the ride through deserts, forests, to the sea,
the big beyond observed from a white beach
like a glass door into the sky,
a space her voice is always aimed into,
elusive, blue, and riding out of reach.

LOVING THAT MAN OF MINE

The timing's flawless. When she meets the phrase
it's like a line considered by the heart
so long it colours phrasing. Mauve to blue.

Bringing it out and turning notes is like
biting into an orange by the sea
and testing loneliness. He never cares
or will according to her need,
the fur coat, perfumes, hardly mean a thing
to a torch singer spotlit at the mike
bleeding the texture of a song.

And song's about the flaw we never mend,
the inequalities in love,
the mistimings, seeing him walk away
into the big unknown one rainy night.

She won't go offstage any happier,
but for a moment somatizes loss,
head cradled in one hand, the other up,
a brooch catching fire at the throat
and when the song cuts she's still travelling
the deep hurts back to an expiring note.

Travelling

Dressed in red feathers in an open car,
this is America, the highway dust
bitches chrome finishes, a side-on bar

dips into register, is blown away
like small town incidentals in a film.
The woman breezed about as Lady Day

sits reading Gershwin lyrics. She's asleep
or hooking at consciousness, this and that
are flashbacks streaming through out of a deep

unconscious autonomy. Foot down hard,
the white convertible makes a U-turn
sending wired chickens squalling through a yard,

a redneck farmer levelling a gun.
The driver tilts his hat back from his head,
grey clouds split open to an orange sun.

She wants to picnic by the maple wood,
slow time down for an afternoon, the band
lazing in her conciliating mood,

the whole group elbow-propped in bitty grass.
They drink from asbestos cups. Lady Day
cradles her wine in the one stolen glass,

a 3-star fixture. They are on the way
across a continent. She stabs a heel
clean through a beetle twinkling on L.A.,

the scored map lifting on the sudden breeze.
She crawls after it, and the others whoop
like crazy Indians running through the trees.

BILLIE'S BLUES

Three white gardenias in her cobalt hair
she's all palpable feeling under wraps
as though her voice placed bruises on the air,

little reminders that won't go away.
She leaves her accompanists vamp, and takes
a taxi ride between songs, it's her way,

a ritual chill-out around Central Park.
Lady, in a red satin gown, laid back,
shoes kicked off, cruising through the abstract dark

in touch with her inconsolable pain,
suspicious of the colour of her skin.
The road blazes with sudden, violent rain.

Her phrasing's always just behind the beat,
the band fill in windows each time she breathes
or shifts expression, and she goes to meet

their tempo, slowly, drawlish, dead on right.
She hardly moves, her voice does everything.
She's isolated in a white spotlight.

She's singing of burning flesh in 'Strange Fruit',
slaves hung on whistling meat-hooks, and the way
the different are permitted no root

from which to grow into identity.
She lets it go, moves offstage, changes gown,
still finger-snapping to the melody.

Reach For the Stars

Money and time, she fists them to a paste.
The zipper on her gown gets jammed,
a notched gap in a straight-run waterfall.
Backstage the flowers are a crammed assault –

a shock statement of red roses,
and all those illegible fan letters,
requests for numbers. When the world stops dead,
it's for the pin-light, not a mountain fire.

Everyone tells her the desert is black,
wait there long enough and the one blows through,
forgotten love dressed up in chains,
face clinging to redundant seventeen.

Singing to her's like frying an omelette,
watching emotions scramble in the pan
to be directed by a pitch
so narrow it touches on everything

with such a blue consistency.
Life, she will tell you, is so rarely lived,
it's the two minutes of a song
edited into unreality.

Nothing but the jazz-pool. Stoned musicians,
a closed, hermetic order. Lester Young,
blowing a horn and off the wall,
sleepwalking in a crumpled suit.

She won't forget her lines. They're on her breath.
Another gown breathes on her back.
Things get assembled, like a year's fan-mail
left in a room somewhere as a white stack.

BILLIE'S NOVEL IN TEN CHAPTERS

Chapter One

Sometimes it rains, and that's a small comment about the big. The sky is swimming. Red, white and black fish nose in and out of the clouds. Tomorrow's hung with black drapes in another place, another town. Carmen McRae once said of me:

> 'Singing is the only place she can express herself the way she'd like to be all the time. Only way she's happy is through a song. I don't think she expresses herself as she would want to when you meet her in person. The only time she's at ease and at rest with herself is when she sings.'

I met somebody in a town. I left my hotel room and went out for a long walk. Or rather I walked autonomously, my direction chosen for me, as though there were arrows on the pavement which corresponded to pre-coded nervous impulses. I placed my feet in spaces that my mind had chosen.

There were crystalline blocks on a construction site. They looked like they had fallen out of the sky. Faces had crystallized in their mineral planes. The building going up showed clouds travelling across its empty windows.

I was on a chemically charged perambulation. Who was it had filled my arms with dead flowers? Dead red-black roses. As though I was a bride turning up to marry absence in a cemetery by the river. I once saw coffins floating down the spine of the Hudson. A whole navigating flotilla of black coffins, drifting towards a woman waving her arms on the opposite shore.

I kept on walking. I don't know how it got there, but there was a lighthouse at the end of the street. Its red eye stared at me like absolute redemption. I went straight towards it, listening to the staccato click of my spike heels on the pavement. And when I reached the place, there was a man with his collar up draped around the white column. It was only a lamppost, but the man was real. He looked at me like I was someone else.

Chapter Two

When we got to the hotel, I was remembering something else that had been written about me. You know, you never see yourself on stage, and if you could you'd be dead. To get outside your head in a wraparound circular motion and look in is the art of astral visualization.

'On stage she was free of extravagant gestures, she swayed her body slightly, crooked her right arm and kept time by moving it in a restrained circular motion snapping her fingers in tempo; the audience rarely took their eyes off her.'

He rarely took his eyes off me. I could feel the silk stockings breathing on my legs. When the elevator came down it was full of sand and shells, as though the sea had come this far just once, and deposited gold on the blue carpeted floor.

Something had got into these compression doors, and the hotel I found myself in was different to the one in which I had left my minks and satin stage gowns. When we got into the lift, the man said, 'Don't worry, the sea doesn't usually come this far in a city. Sometimes dimensions get changed round, and no-one knows where they are. I'm James Dean,' he said, and his gelled hair broke from its immobility, and a forelock brushed his left eye. 'I don't know whether it's you who are here, or I, but I know we can't both be on the same dimension.'

We got out at the fourth floor. All the doors to rooms were open. A woman in the form of a violet hologram blinked down the corridor. Her fluent audiovisual body disappeared on its trans-personal plane. It was as though I had entered an amnesia fugue.

'Call me Jimmy,' my guide said. I was suddenly weightless, dissociated. Our being here clicked as though we were on a telepathic microfilm. I was no longer walking but floating.

Jimmy took me into a red, cavernous ballroom. There was a crashed car in the middle of the floor as a central exhibit. He pointed to the jagged, concertinaed metal, diamonded by impacted shards of glass. He opened the unhinged backdoor, and said, 'marry me in my death.'

Chapter Three

When you're on the road, anything can happen. Buses with their headlights tunnelling through fog, limousines in which I take smack, a big blue sky suddenly boiling with thunder, it's all part of a continuing travelogue. I forget everything except that sustained moment in which a note lengthens. I want to report on myself again in someone else's words.

'. . . Then Fred Robbins introduced her, all in black, a little black lace here and there, the skirt slit at the front showed her legs when she moved. White gloves long with no fingers, just caught around the thumbs. Her hair in a twisted and unbraided coronet on top of her head. She turned to the pianist and announced her numbers *sotto voce* . . . all with that seesaw motion of the arms, fingers always turned in, that swanlike twitching of the thighs, that tortured posture of the head, those inquiring eyes, a little frightened at first and then as the applause increased they became grateful.'

That's me under a spotlight. A blue voice. I'd like to die on my feet singing 'I Cover the Waterfront'. In a dark blue gown.

When I got back to the streets, the lighthouse was gone. There was a spiral tear in my left stocking. I was earthed again. A child came towards me, his eyes directed at a point of focus over my shoulder, but his feet making a clear line to intersect with my own. I wasn't frightened. He was carrying a blue box with gold stars splashed on the sides. A taxi sped down the white road, but the child walked clean through it. The person in the rear of the taxi threw their head round, but it was too late, and they were already a hundred miles down the road. The child continued walking towards me, clutching his blue box. I stopped dead. There was a scorpion inside the container, and a splash of jewels. Paste rubies and sapphires. The child left the box in my hands. I walked with it a while, and hummed 'Lover Man' and it dematerialized. The road turned blue. All the way to the stars.

Chapter Four

Loneliness is tangential to my life. It shows up on an inner display. I open doors into long vertical drops. My past is down there, my mother the duchess sits in the void with marguerites building around her like white constellations. When I try to reach her it's like film. There's the image, but nobody's there. What do you do with the broken-hearted? They live in a blue desert in the middle of the city. There are mirrors surrounding this inner city. They can never see out, they can only reflect themselves.

Johnny Guarnieri once said: 'Looking back, I would say that few performers had such solid judgement about tempo as she did, particularly when it came to doing certain tunes in a very slow tempo. Most performers who try the slow-tempo bit do it for effect, not because it's right for the tune. Billie Holiday was the greatest tempo singer that ever lived.'

I was still walking around a complex of streets, none of which carried names, or were identifiable. I thought I knew the town, like you remember something when a foghorn wails off the coast, and your childhood comes back like a white butterfly blown into the hands.

I wanted to buy some stockings. Silk ones, with a cuban heel and seams. All the shop windows were empty. It hadn't occurred to me that there weren't any crowds. It was like singing after the music has stopped, and being unaware of it. There was a window-dresser in one of the shops arranging a wide-brimmed purple hat on a mannequin. There was a net and feather complementing the creation. I was astounded because the mannequin was black. When I saw the hat I knew instantly that it was for me. It was my sort of style. Lady Day in purple. Her toenails painted green. I tapped on the glass, and the girl turned around. She was my idea of a dream. I pressed my lips to the glass, and she hers, and together we simulated a passionate kiss, the oval rotation of one tongue extracting the anthered life-source from another. Love, desperate love on the outside looking in.

Chapter Five

Where do you go after making love to the dead? I was still in this town without a name, looking for the club in which I would sing at night. I had the songs on access, codified in my memory cells, not like when I've shot up and retrieving them is like breaking holes in the frozen American lakes to pull out fish. I'm always in behind the beat, but sometimes I'm so far back as to be shadow-singing in a parallel dimension. My husbands write to me in my dreams. An oneiric subtext in which they profess love. But love is the stranger who follows me from town to town. He leaves snow on my bed and roses. He demateri-alizes each time I open my eyes. When they're shut, he writes his name on the outstretched palms of my hands.

> I like reading about myself. It tells me the past really does exist. 'A certain kind of guy really appealed to her, it was like a pretty chick in high school – if anyone warns her to stay away from so-and-so they're pushing her starting button. If there was one guy in a crowded room who was tough, and mean, and meant trouble, then Lady would find him. There were a lot of bruises in Billie's life, and I just didn't understand all that.'

I kept on searching. Dead alleys, a side-street in which what looked like my old pea-green Cadillac was parked, a public square in which tables laid with black cloths were grouped under a spread of giant plane trees. There was no-one there. The cafés were boarded up. A single column of fog stood in the precinct. I had the feeling there was somebody behind my thoughts. A light on inside. When I heard the Cadillac driven away, I could see there was nobody at the wheel. The car was empty. I was still looking for the club, and wondering if the musicians had already found it. But then the window-dresser was there. I saw her very clearly, dressed in a black raincoat with the collar turned up, and heard her red heels snapping on the pavement. She was unlocking the door to one of the houses overlooking the square. She must have lived there. My heart jolted with the need to know this girl. But then I realized we were in different towns. I would have had to cross a continent to cross a square. But I was remem-bering my songs for another opening night. 'I Cover the Waterfront . . .'

Chapter Six

Where do we go when we don't want to be ourselves? I don't know why I'm the only audience in this cinema. My blue mink sits on me like a microclimate. Needle marks score my skin, like eschatological pointillism. When you arrive somewhere you don't always remember where you came from. Usually, when I get to a hotel I spend the time making up. A fixation with putting on a face. This time it's not necessary. My face stays on. There's been a wedding in this town. Confetti spots the pavement. There's a white wedding dress and veil discarded on the bonnet of a black limo. Was it the window-dresser's? Did she secretly marry another woman and run out on her? What you do belongs to you, but it's also a habit, the involuntary stream of being.

'Occasionally, she played cards or listened to records with the musicians, but more often she relaxed in her own room watching television or listening to the radio. If she was wearing an elaborate hairstyle then hours would be spent with its coiffure; at one time when she wore her hair in tight curls she would sit in front of the mirror crimping with an old-fashioned curling iron. She always carried more earrings, bracelets and necklaces than she ever needed, and her preference for neatness showed in the way she carefully arranged everything in her hotel rooms.'

It's going to rain, and I still haven't found the club. The chestnut leaves are opening their fans in anticipation of the downpour. I can hear a sax wailing in the clouds. An apocalyptic invocation to storm. I've come to live my life by rhythm. Even in my dreams I'm trying to discern the beat. And here at last is somebody. A man wearing mirror shades, a green jacket, and berry-polished black pointed shoes, comes strolling through an avenue of trees. He checks the cloud level. His leisurely manner of walking suggests he's headed nowhere. But I watch him come on like kinetic flotation. If he's part of a dream, then so am I. But now a driving rain obscures the scene. A solid crystal wall intervenes between us. We're two fish swimming in a fluid jewel. We'll never meet, and the air's turned into a lake.

Chapter Seven

I live in states of altered consciousness. Something or someone keeps drawing me to the river. Eddie lives there. When I saw him last his arms were spotted like a leopard. I wanted to place Eddie in my novel, but he's resisted inclusion. He's someone else in words. He's not the same Eddie, who counts the boats going down the river. They're his friends, even if they are always going away towards foreign skylines. Ships disappear through blue windows on the other side of the world. Eddie gives me things like words, understanding, sailor's hats, grapefruits, flotsam and dreamshapes that he keeps in biscuit tins. When ships go by his window, he calls them angels. He invests them with mystique. Eddie dyes his hair magenta. He sleeps in a ship's bunk in a room decorated like a cabin. All my life I've had a dependency on male dominance. Eddie's something different. He touches me lightly, as though his fingertips were eyelashes. What do they say of Billie?

'I turned my life over to John. He took all my money, I never had any money, we were supposed to get married. I went into my room. John closed the door behind me. Then someone grabbed me and threw me against the wall. I never smoked opium in my life. John told me to throw some trash away. I did it. My man makes me wait on him, not him on me. I never did anything without John telling me, that's all I know.'

Eddie would like to live on a harbour front, surrounded by ships in dry-dock. Liners, tankers, tugs, fishing vessels, small craft. He gets high on the marine tang of oil, hemp, rust, iodine. He dresses like a sailor, and tells me he can produce anchor-shaped tears. When we walk by the river together, we talk of dreams. Eddie says there's a big book buried on the shore of a desert island, in which all the great secrets are disclosed. The book is written by the wind. Eddie likes to think these things. He'd like to believe the shore is star-dust. When we go back, we play records and drink tumblers of Cutty Sark. Eddie puts on my earrings. There's a moon up so big it could topple the buildings. We hear a ship's horn out there in the liquid silk. It's the loneliest sound in the world. It makes me want to sing 'Jim' or 'Solitude'.

Chapter Eight

A shoot-out at the Attucks Hotel. Bullets impacted the car's windows as we got away. The police wanted me on any terms. A fiction introduced into a fiction? In the end no-one separates reality from unreality. It depends on which hemisphere of the brain you favour: right or left-side dominance. A singer stands at a microphone between the two.

Everything becomes narrative. We consume our own process. When I sing I eat my life by the tail. I call it catching snakes. The loop. The oroborous. No way out under the spotlight. Injecting subjective biography into an existing melody is a trap. It shifts old patterns in the listener, but doesn't help the singer. Eddie's better off watching ships slide by on the tidal current. He goes with them. He travels their way. I stay on my breath. Eddie likes the orange-hulled Norwegian tankers putting out on a long thalassic haul. The ones that go through windows. And my timing?

'The band's been there since 12 o'clock, and they're ready to pack up but the company's taken the place till 3, so they sit there . . . So we walk in at 20 minutes after 2 and she goes to the ladies' room. And she came in at 20 minutes to 3 and we were done at 10 minutes to 3. And those are the records you hear now.'

The records. They're already posthumous from the first take. I try to hear myself as I would if I were dead. I mean with fractional delay. If the dead exist they make some sort of synchronistic intersection with sound. A singer needs to think that. Eddie says he hears the wail of ships' horns even when asleep. One voyage contacting another, his mauve hair spread like a sea anemone on the pillow. And people keep a voice in their head when they're walking around, thinking, sitting alone outside a café, or just wanting consolation for a down mood. I can be heard all over the continent in silence. I'm played on a neural wave. Listen for Billie, and she's on the inside. Eddie likes strawberries. He eats them slowly, while he's looking out for ships in the night. He says they go by like fortresses. All lit up in the dark. When I hear myself singing it's like that. I'm in the notes which are yours as you hear them. Eddie sleeps alone at his bedroom window, and the fog blows bluely by.

Chapter Nine

When I woke up I had aged ten years. Or was it ten years since I had last checked my mirror? My body clock mutates according to cellular rhythm. There's someone in my bed and her name is Sandy. Her perfume flashes into my association: Chanel No 5. It smells of Hollywood opulence, and recalls blondes pouting in red lipstick, furs warming to the leather interiors of stretch Cadillacs. Sandy's been compulsively coming backstage after the shows. Big-eyed, and lit up by some shape-lifting inner current. I'd like to make up a story for her before she wakes. Sandy comes from a family in the stars. She can't get back there, but she's always looking up at the sky. They'll arrive one night, and take her back. If she opened her eyes while she was sleeping, you'd see two stars. One for each pupil. Sandy eats strawberry ice-cream and has strawberry hair. But I'm still curious about myself.

> 'She was one of the kindest people I ever knew, and the outward manifes-tation of harshness and being tough was only a compensatory mechan-ism for an inferiority complex. Few people really knew Lady because she never allowed herself to get close to people.'

Sandy looks bruised by passion. The black spaghetti straps on her negligée have slipped down from her shoulders. I'm mostly somewhere else. Maybe we met ten years ago, and she's still here with me. My jewels catch light and spill at her throat. Or perhaps Sandy has materialized from a dream. She may have sleepwalked out of my forehead, and now she'll never get back inside, unless I dream her back to my interior. Fans and lovers show up anywhere and every-where. They break down all the barriers. Or did I meet Sandy with Eddie? Sandy and I must have walked along the shore, counting stars as they show in the sea, and nipping bourbon from the bottle. I remember a ship shone clear on the horizon. It was silver and transmitted an intense radial luminosity. It wasn't one of Eddie's ships, and I don't think he even saw it. He was busy picking up a polished shard of green glass, busy dabbing his fingers in the water. But Sandy and I saw it. It was like the new day. And now tomorrow, it's ten years on. Ten years later.

Chapter Ten

I carry a torch in my heart and in my fist. It's the light that screens a singer from the audience. It's the lit square in my heart across which I chase my childhood. Perhaps a huge green fish will jump out of the fountain, and bring me news of the dead. I've performed in so many cities, and this is the only one whose name I have forgotten. I can't find my blue Lincoln, with my stash in the glove compartment. I can't find the club where I'm to sing in the back of the sky. When you're near to death, they say you hear a child singing in the dark. If Eddie or the window-dresser or the black mannequin were to show up, they could point me the way to the club. Six pernods with brandy floaters, and I'm ready to modulate breath at the microphone. So many things are said to me. I'm fragmented into multiple simulacra.

'Sometimes you listen to a performer, and every fibre of that performer's body seems to be incorporated in what she is doing. It's not only the voice, you feel that what the person is saying or singing comes from the inner-most depths of her being – this was one of Billie's characteristics, and that is the thing which endures in the minds of people who remember her.'

Perhaps I've always been dead. I would like to have sat on one of the flotilla of coffins navigating down the Hudson. I would have awoken on another shore. There would have been a rusty anchor hanging in the sky, and a procession dressed in red travelling away from the reality-grid. Billie's Blues? They'll be heard always as their primal roots are twisted into the heart's ventricles. If Eddie shows up in the rain, he'll be carrying a ship in a bottle. He'll say 'Sis, I told you you shouldn't get lost in places like this. You're in the wrong time and place. Let's go back to the river, and find a bar and listen to the ships going down the river. That way, we'll be on one of them heading South.'

It's going to rain again. Migrational swarms of flashing drops. An atmospheric orchestration; a scherzo. I'll find the club in the end. It will be dark inside. I will only see the microphone. I'll make my way backstage. Dry ice. Red fog. The big possibilities. Absolute concentration. I'm on again. It feels like I'm talking, but I'm singing. Eddie's sitting at a table. He'll wait for me afterwards, and take me back to the river. I want to go that way for ever.

BRUISING NOTES BLUE

My lips my
heart my shoes
my love my
grief my loss
my heart my
bluely broken heart
my breath my
space my emptiness
my toes my
seams my memory
my cells my
bluely broken heart
my pitch my
phrasing my poise
my timing my
mystery my death
my moment my
bluely broken heart
my again my
blackly broken heart
my again my
redly broken heart
my again my
bluely broken heart
my tongue my
you my me
my temerity my
nerves my irreverence
my mink my
tone my leave
my up my
down my wound
my again my
bluely broken heart
my notes my
bruising lyric blue

Bringing Style To Pain

She'd cut her heart out to erase the pain,
segment it into six melon canoes.
Honey, my pearls are melting in the rain.

It starts with gospel, waters underground
reverberating through a smoky throat.
Honey, I'm singing when I make no sound.

At twelve, women stand on a chair and sing,
their shyness concentrated into power.
Honey, my finger's nagging for a ring.

There's always rain at night. A lover gone,
a dead parent floating across the dark.
Honey, I'm breaking up inside, alone.

Mostly in love, the other cuts a scar
so deep, it never heals along a seam.
Honey, I dazzle as a burnt-out star.

Everything breaks up. Black boats in a dream
unloading coffins full of saxophones.
Honey, I'm blindfold sitting by the stream.

They're sisters of the night, the ones who find
consolatory notes in their damaged lives.
Honey, you'll break my fingers if I'm kind.

She cut her heart out, set the thing on fire,
ran with it in both hands across the street.
Honey, it's love and death that I desire.

Coming Out

Blue conifers. The oak's dense like a lake,
a concentrated bump of chlorophyll.
A year inside, she hasn't sung a word,
her voice is subterranean, a stone
she fears she's let sink in a stagnant pool
roofed over by flotillas of dead leaves.

They've driven her to Bobby Tucker's farm,
the place is being licked with two-tone paint.
She raids old cases for a white silk gown,
comes down, the piano's been moved to the porch,
an ebony Steinway, so highly strung
it seems to resonate with melody.

She throws her head back from the bourbon's hit,
her first pacifying explosive shot
that's like walking on stage again, the fast
rush of adrenalin. A second shot,
a blue jay screams in the leaf canopy,
and instinctively she kicks off her shoes

and hears Bobby's free-basing medley hint
at something in her dormant repertoire,
a polyrhythmic throw at 'Night and Day'.
Energy catches fire between her toes,
she lifts and bounces on her stockinged feet
and feels the breath travel along her spine,

establish space inside her chest and throat
and everything she sees is indigo,
a blue surrounding mauve, a deepening tone
enhancing clarity – it's hers to stay,
a first, a second note, the effortless
return to singing as she holds on 'day'.

BRENDA

A rich white heiress from Fifth Avenue,
she keeps getting backstage, raindropped with jewels,
spooking a closed space, she is high with charge
like someone swimming out and out
on overreach into the deep,
eyes dark blue like the water in that place
jolting a cold vortical grip.
She fills a silk stocking with dollar notes
and sequins, pins it with a rose,

and leaves it for Miss Holiday
the anomie-mystique of Lady Day.
And all the modish butch accessories
she chooses, men's jackets and suits

arrive in tissues and are left untouched.
Brenda, haunting Café Society,
compelled to keep returning every night,
fixated, confiscating every word
as though the phrase was written for her heart,

sips obsessively at cocktails,
trying to draw attention to the wound
that makes her special, unrequited love
with all its poisonous, smoking lakes,

its crying out all summer for a hand.
Each night she dresses more flamboyantly,
occupies a table alone,
pours drinks for two, and stares up at the stage,
agonized, dejected, hearing the band
change tempo, and the singer drop
a low register and walk off in a rage.

Couldn't I

Amazingly recherché, a red suite
windowed on to a blue Swiss lake,
the swans are clouds on clouds dipping the film,
and if I dropped here from the sky
the touch-down never broke my dream,
the concert happened, it was hours ago
I stepped right through a mirror to myself
as a total identity
all silks and theatricalized gestures,

my gown rippling with all those eyes
and all those eyes. A detonative stage.
Upwards of forty I don't count the years,
it's easier to dream of youth,
live backwards in this cushioning
of fluffy snow on snow

a blue zero.
Couldn't I run out naked to the day
fisting out diamonds on my skin
a scattered glitter all over
a rainbow dazzle on my lips
dancing to the edge of the ice?

How many stairs in a dead waterfall?
A pair of shoes on every ledge?
I lie in bed. The window is the sky,
no seam in that transparency,

a bruised red sun trembles right on the edge.

Chasing Chickens in Satin Lipstick

New York's a poem with a vocal line,
a surreal artefact in which new stars
are cloned in a high silver loft,
each week more supernovae hit the street
with purple laces, snakeskin shoes,
a programmed formula, a zany beat.
I tighten life into my mitt,
I'll meet my past somewhere in a side-street,
the litter bins spilling paste jewels
into a turquoise gutter. I'll be leaning out
the window opposite the cinema
waiting for life to start, waiting all day
to be given my part. 'That's you,'
they'll say, and I'll begin. That's me.
Sometimes I have this crazy urge
to chase purple chickens around the room,
they'd be a different colour on the farm.
Purple chickens lay purple eggs.
These days I use my lower vocal register,
my options hardly rising above speech.
It sets a style, the way limitations
in time grow to a cult. My room is dark.
I put my hand out to arrest a cloud
beyond the open window, pull it in.
I'll travel to a movie, see myself
in a small part. Really I'm far away,
elbows on the window sill, looking out
for handsome blue-eyed love to come my way.

HEY, MISTER

Death came to visit me. His eyes were gold.
He snapped my picture through a violet lens.
My name was added to the microfiche.
That day snow blew around the liquor store
studded with candles. There was someone there
behind the someone there. It's nobody,
only two eyes stepped into the big cloud,
nervy, inquisitive, and fixed on me.
Letters keep falling from my shopping bag,
they multiply like rectangles of snow,
a blowy, proliferating blizzard,
all written over, Lady Day.
The agent is sitting outside in the car,
the car is sitting inside my head,
the agent is in the car. It's afternoon,
a time when singers sleep. They've caught me out;
I should be washed by waters of a dream,
a dark green tidal current on which ships
go wandering into amnesia.
Floppy red and blue flags waving from clouds.
The agent has got eyes all over his skin
like raindrops picked up from a thunderstorm.
Death's nearer. He's got my blueprint
and not my fingerprints. My DNA.
The bottle turns to an intractable
glacier and shatters on the floor.
I really don't know who will get me first,
the owner asks me for my autograph,
takes out a long-poled broom and sweeps the store.

SAINT BILLIE

She brings you every permutation of emotive eloquence. She talks behind you even when distraction takes you somewhere else. Her low-light locale's a club and the unconscious. You think she's in the studio, wearing a dress from Abercrombie and Fitch, her lipline a diva's mulberry arch, you think she's there in off-the-elbow gloves, but the CD cut out hours ago. She goes on singing out of time. We've all got Billie in our memory cells. Saint Billie on aural recall.

Lady in a blue Burberry? Like Leonard Cohen's famous blue raincoat. It's raining over St Sulpice, St Germain, the ports of Hamburg and Amsterdam. St Catherine's docks. A pointillistic shawl. Someone standing on the harbour sees an angel fly over. The angel is silver and explodes into an irradiating super-nova. Seagulls hang out in the matt-white sky.

Imagine a meeting between Saint Jean Genet and Saint Billie Holiday. Two legendized icons meeting in an alley. The drain cover turns gold. Someone leaning out of an open window, throws a red rose down between them. They are both humiliated by their origins, which are simple. They are connected by roots which travel deep like an oak tree's across the radius of a field. At the base of those roots are poverty and genius. These are ineradicable foundations to their respective creative autonomies. Neither belongs to any social or ideological grouping. They have themselves as the dictate to a particular expression. The neuronal halo surrounding their meeting is violet tipped with blue. They don't even know each other's names. The meeting's a self-deconstructing illusion. It's like the union of two holograms. The polarisation is intense and evanescent. Saint Billie leaves a black glove in Saint Jean's hand. What he imparts is a gesture of the sadness which is inseparable from his eyes. He knows sadness as a commonplace of consciousness like light. When he looks back there is nobody there. When she looks back there are lilacs spilling over a wall, purple tusks which seem to have sprung out of the instant, like a thought showing up big in memory. She goes to a bar. He goes to a bar. All the lights blow for a moment. Then the song begins.

THE BILLIE NO-ONE KNEW

The woman inside the performer. She is someone fighting for her life behind the scenes, invoking the simplicity of childhood poverty, cleaning bathrooms in antebellum houses and working in a brothel. That woman won't recede into the forest. She's had to adopt a secondary role. She courted fame too young, and got burnt by the illusion of money and success. She's still sitting, skirt above her knees, in the sunlight on the porch. Looking out into the ordinary day. Baltimore in a red sunset. Her mother crying over being left, and cursing her rival in the kitchen. Eleanora. Where is she now? She had to change her name into an unidentifiable opposite.

Eleanora had Billie escape once before a concert at the Hi-Hat Club in Boston. Neither could be found. They'd got into a car and been driven out to the forest. There were big oaks and maples overspilling a field with cobalt shadow. The place was concentrated viridian. There were bluejays in the high branches, and an alphabet of gnats spotting by the gate to a field. The car was left parked and waiting, the driver with his head cradled on the headrest, and Billie walking the distance to the gate to meet Eleanora. Billie held out her arm for her invisible other to take. It was like retrieving youth and walking towards the new day. All the self-dissolution of the older woman absolved, her spirit rejuvenated by Eleanora's remedial hand. Billie was happy for just those moments. The light streamed through her cells. There was a smell of child-hood cooking as though the past was right there in the centre of a field. She was regressing to a state of trance. She sat down in the raffish grasses under a tree, and talked down the years. She kicked off her high heels, and injected *alla breve* into the chorus of 'Too Marvellous For Words'. But there was something missing. The past was no more tangible than the future. She was isolated by abstract configurations. A black beetle flitted across her stockinged foot. Eleanora was chasing away into the marble forest. She had shed her white dress and Billie picked it up in despair, reacquainting herself with childhood smells. She walked back to the car like a deserted bride. She had betrayed and been betrayed. The driver was still asleep. She was performing that night. She still had the white dress in her arms. It was flecked with ink-stains. The man drove all the way back to Boston without opening his eyes.

JOHNNY SQUARE AND GINA CUBE

They're listening to the Complete Verve Recordings. Gina sits in a pink cocktail skirt, and Johnny's not sure if he should be Scarlet today. Sometimes Scarlet demands too much. Her intense parodic femininity requires saturative attention. Scarlet's sulking in the wardrobe. Johnny's concerned the lake outside might finally crawl through the window. It's the colour of malachite today or ivy arresting the turrets of a ruined château. Johnny and Gina have slept through a whole week with their eyes open on nothing. It's a sort of inverted wave function. Johnny worries that Billie has escaped through a hole in the quantum foam which interconnects all regions of space-time. He worries that she could have disappeared to the dead.

Johnny Square and Gina Cube. They sit opposite each other in leopard-skin armchairs. The moon is up in the afternoon. Billie liked singing 'Wishing on the Moon'. Gina's bought some new purple spike heels. She keeps on taking them out of their tissue in the box and admiring their aesthetic qualities. Billie's singing 'I'll Never Smile Again'. Scarlet feels like that today. She's not going to come out. Johnny imagines himself leaning moodily over the railings on a hotel terrace, the bikinied beach girls looking up at him, and he averting his eyes, putting on dark glasses and walking away. His archetypal eat your heart out fantasy. And twenty minutes later he would appear as Scarlet and have the men throw their eyes over their shoulders.

They each sit visualizing Billie according to their own respective needs. If Johnny could bring his Billie out of his head she wouldn't fit into Gina's. They would represent two very different psychic cut-outs. One wouldn't necessarily be recognizable to the other. If Billie could step out of Johnny's head, she would be broken-hearted, consummately stylized, a woman singing as though her life depended on each word. And if Billie extrapolated herself from Gina's imagining, she would be a woman more in control. She would be the exploited, but positively resilient character who rises above male dominance. There would be more emphasis on the person than the image. But the two continue to sit and listen. Johnny Square and Gina Cube. The lake knocks at the window, but it doesn't come in. It leaves three star-shaped plane leaves stuck to the glass. Johnny and Gina relax as the night comes on. The moon was shining in the afternoon, now the sun comes out of the night. It's all the same to them, and anything can happen.

SAHARA BLUE

Mostly my dead go there. Mother's still frying chicken for the hard luck stories in a squiffy mirage. Lester Young keeps going and coming back, like he can't decide to die properly. He raises a trumpet to the sky and appraises his destiny. The notes that escape turn into vultures and angels. He takes a step back and teleports himself into the city. Another lonely hotel room with a bottle of Jack Daniels on the bedside table. I too approach the frontier. There's a car out there partly buried in the white sands. It's the colour of my old Lincoln. A rusting carapace half dug in like a stranded turtle on the shoreline. The radio's still playing inside.

When I'm crossing the continent I imagine deserts. Rats the size of horses scurry across the sands at night. The near stars are brilliantly close-up, like a necklace picked out by a pin-light when I sing 'Strange Fruit' right at the end, a finale begging no encore. In their minds, the audience sees me swinging from a Southern tree. I see carbonized forests obtruding from the desert. And if you go far enough towards nowhere you have to arrive somewhere. Jazz is like that. Giving form to inchoate emotions. How many of the audience pick on the singer, rather than the song? They somatically visualize before they hear. And that way the singer becomes more important than the song. Lady Day about to collapse or be led offstage by a minder.

Do You Know Orange From Red

Billie's out shopping for dresses and lingerie. She lacks money. Where it goes is unaccountable. There's a hand takes it all away, and anyhow there's a weird relationship between singing and what it buys. How does a voice translate itself into a rail of silks and satins? Billie's eye was acquisitively kleptomaniacal. She wanted everything with a sense of omniverous possession. Her need was to be loaded with ostentatious purchases. And back home she would view them with a sense of culpable dispassion. An aggressive detachment that would have her swear to put an end to compulsive buying. And it seemed odd and maladjusted to her at times, that she was in a big department store by virtue of the pain in her voice. The two seemed to have no juxtapositional meeting point. It was like life and death. They shouldn't be on the same train, but they are.

Billie brings her purchases back to her apartment. Cashmere and lamb's wool jumpers, skirts, perfumes, silk stockings.

She can hear a conversation in the sky. Someone's asking if they should go on or turn back. Whoever it is, is on the way to dying, but hasn't completed the journey. She returns down a white tunnel to her temporal identity. Billie is so anxious over the voices, she calls a friend. She needs reassurance. She runs her fingers over the cool silks she has purchased. She tries on her silk lingerie. The night's blowing in outside. Lights come on in adjoining blocks, yellow interiors showing up all over the city. Billie's loneliness is just one register in the scale of encompassing solitude. She stares at the television screen like it's an underwater artefact brought to the surface. It's another dimension eluding her sense of the real. Everything's on film in the external world. She can walk from one take to another. It looks like the stars are falling. Supernovae imploding across consciousness. She returns to trying on clothes. Her show isn't until midnight. She looks at dress after dress. Black, white, blue and red. She can't choose between an orange and a red. She decides for herself and not for the reverse of her pigment. It's getting bluer, blacker outside. A woman in the opposite apartment slides out of her dress. Billie admires her tomato-red bra. She's snatching at the same television show. They each feed on unreality like a salad. Billie chooses red. In the car ride to the club she ages two thousand years.

LOVER MAN

He hangs a black silk jacket on the door,
a fetishistic prelude, white shirt sleeves;
the whip's coiled like a cobra on the floor.

A snaky man, his eyes jump at my skin,
my need's the epicentre to his own,
a zebra stripe shows where the lash cuts in.

He takes his tie off, appraises the grain
my body represents lying face down,
each site registers its degree of pain.

It's a pre-show ritual. He beats me hard
to season my delivery. The dark
sits like a cat with ears pricked in the yard.

He tells me I won't make the show tonight,
the torchy Queen of 52nd Street,
whose instincts counterpoint this rocky fight.

I'm trodden on, and learn beneath the heel
how in the end bright suns go chasing through.
It's only through extremes I learn to feel.

He leaves me dress. I patch up a blue eye.
I run the tap, sapphires dance in the steam,
the water's blue like a Pacific sky.

And love is in the air. I start to glow
with channels I'll communicate on stage
talking my wound out and keeping it low.

WEIRD AND CLEAR

She dreams of rivers, and a hazy day
disconnected from time. A suitcase floats
along the current's grabbing spine,
a red dress tugging free in the journey

she wore once at the Storyville,
flaming silk gone down river to the source.
She speeds on the jumpy autonomy,
her father's waiting for her on the shore,

a rusty trumpet raised towards the sun.
Drinks in a club later with Lester Young,
she slips in and out of sleep all the day
still wearing high heels on the hotel bed.

She's back somewhere in a building's cellar,
searching for clues left behind as a child,
a ballet shoe, a comic book, a pin,
a voice dictating rhythm in her head,

the vague notion that everything she had
would get concentrated into her breath,
arms out, and slightly raised, the scatty child
interrogates a clear jewel in her sex.

She's sleeping through appointments, rehearsals,
everything last night plays back weird and clear,
the stage is like an island lost at sea,
the lighthouse blinks a red eye in the fog.

She surfaces, reluctant to let go
her father's impromptu riff, and he drops
down to one knee – the fog is blowing in –
raises his left hand and the music stops.

I Didn't Know What Time It Was

And love breaks every moment in her heart. The rainy season, so many autumns washed up at the interior. Ships come home to winter in the heart.

She puts on dark glasses and goes out to the avenue. The sky's a poem when you're in love, and a big indomitable blank curve when you're alone. She walks her love the length of the avenue. An adopted afternoon mystique. 'I want to die,' she tells herself, 'but only if I can retain the little pleasures I have in life.' And a second later, 'I want to live to have him make things right.' Life's always like film noir. Other people's loves have the imaginary taste of black pepper sprinkled on strawberries. The register's prickly sweet. You see them stepping out of the film in which you live.

She tells herself there's got to be another chance. The perfect stranger. He'll know her like they've always been together. A gold hand in a silver hand. The intuitive flash that things will right themselves. There's a party going on in the sky as it happens. A rainbow wearing purple shoes dances across the sky. Love will set all imbalances to order. Bolts of silk will tumble over waterfalls. The assistant in Bloomingdale's will walk out later to find she's wearing a tiara. Love is the intersection with the marvellous.

And as she walks, her eyes catching at the visuals of shop displays, so someone in a parallel street is also reflecting on the tormenting ramifications of unrequited love. He'll never find his woman, so he buys Billie Holiday records. Her vocal explorations in feeling, in colouring the unspoken, and holding back by implication, are what allows him to empathize with her valedictory tone. He wishes he could impart his troubles to Lady Day, but just by listening to her there's a tenuous union. He would like to buy her some silk stockings and send them backstage. He would like to buy her roses which smell of Paris. He keeps on walking. Walking is like dreaming. You don't really know where you are going. And she is experiencing the same sense of directionless motion. At the end of her mind, as a still undefined parallax, she has the idea she will go to a movie. He too, has the notion of taking refuge from his loneliness in a cinema. He doesn't know it, but his street converges on hers. He walks behind her, paying attention to her legs. Her hair is in a turban, and she's shielded by dark glasses. They enter the same cinema, and sit in the dark.

What Becomes of the Broken Hearted

Billie went to Alaska for two weeks. She would sing a down tempo 'Blue Moon' there. A blue moon over the blazing cold in Alaska. Billie had low-grade viral pneumonia, even though it was summer. Her blue minks had been pawned to pay for a habit. The glacial, abstract light reduced everything to a brutal transparency. A gelid configurative zero. In that sort of bright freeze the mind's contents are turned inside out. You see decades of obsessively recycled images scattered like a random mosaic on the floors. There's a trauma from 1937 as a green jewel twinkling on the ice. 1943 is a glowering ruby hexagram connected by psychic filigree to the implosively shattered mandala. The turquoise splinter belongs to a deep-memory association, and other neural scintillations in the puzzle are scattered across refractive surfaces. She's looking at a prismatic representation of her life. It's all an illusion committed to a telescopic hall of mirrors. Like looking inside a lake in the search for another lake. In Alaska the lakes are all frozen, even if the sky is the blue of a morning-glory.

Billie spends the days trying to pick up coruscating pieces. It's like fishing for jewels. Often, her manager locks her up in the dark all day, and the only food left her for impromptu cooking is a can of chitlins. She's malnutritive. Her stomach has shrunk. She hallucinates delusional states of guilt. She can't protect in love, and she doesn't wish to be protected. She's alone, and everything she assimilates becomes compounded by her voice. That's her way of speaking. Depth clarity in her intonation. 'I'm so scared,' she pleads as she comes out of her locked room. She has no longer any control over her destiny except when she's on stage. The latter is her sanctuary. In Alaska she can believe she is a black slave swinging from a tree, as she concentrates her whole emotive dynamic into the lyrics of 'Strange Fruit'. She never sees any money for her shows.

Blinding, brilliantly unexhilarating cold. She stares into the broken mandala in her hands. Somehow she's accumulated all the pieces. They have a lapidary elusiveness. She likes the dark blue, the green, the red. It might even snow in these colours. She's in withdrawal. It's day, it's night. She's a mirror staring into the eyes of another mirror.

CONVENTION

Bare feet, a woman crosses railway lines
shoes in her hands, then one hand to the sun.
The earth's impacted fire grains underfoot,
and poppies bleed into the undertow.

She's headed for a place where singers go,
an underworld convention, blues cellar,
chthonian studio, where low register
and middle colour to deep indigo.

She finds the stairs, and it's a long way down,
somebody coming up the other way
is right side on, left dematerialized.
The barman's crowded into red sequins.

It's like a dream in which she's strayed into
the shadow side of meaning, round the back
of words and consciousness where things present
their parallels. Her name is Eleanora.

She sits at the bar without questioning
the giant mike on stage. Fruit underfoot
is musty, tropical, its stormy tang
smelling of markets in a Southern port.

That's who and who? It could be Sarah Vaughan
performing aural gymnastics, a phrase
detaches, and circulates like a bee
unaware it's inviting attention.

The faces gathered, won't fully look up,
they seem to lack knowledge of being there.
She places one hand on top of her head
and feels the current crackle in her hair.

Winning and Losing

Sometimes I dream I'm riding on a train
and there's no place I recognize. The light
dazzles along a jolting corridor,
photons punched out of a receding star.

Autumn is reddening over France and Spain,
I tell myself that for information.
If there are other passengers
they must have gone off searching for the bar.

The journey includes mass attacks of trees,
their stormy auburn density
closes at intervals like a tunnel.
The soft creatures drop down on to the roof.

I'm writing a letter to my past,
but the words track across a continent.
Perhaps I'll see you at a small station
boarding a train going the other way.

Winning and losing love, they alternate,
the small town moving one way's standing still.
Two horses pour with sawdust from their sides.
A black car's parked on the near hill,

but nearer, appears turned over.
I deal words but won't get you back,
the ticket collector's eyes are blue snails
attempting to roll down his cheeks

and get away. He says, we're right on time,
but haven't yet done the big bend.
The light keeps arriving from other stars,
of course I'm on this to the very end.

Where Do Icons Go?

She loses herself, and comes back to herself. There's a cypress park at the end of the world, and the sea is beyond it, a lapidary ultramarine. They say if you walk through a blue avenue of trees in the always modified filter of sunlight, then there's a guardian waiting there in a light-tunnel. The biological pace-maker attunes to a para-dimensional rhythm, and after that the getaway is simple. A guardian's hand instead of someone opening the chrome-polished door to a green Cadillac.

But there were other endings. The Mars Club in the rue Saint-Benoit in Montmartre. The singer as narcoleptic somnambulist coming alive in the song, finding equilibrium in Mal Waldron's counterpointing piano. Her voice was like someone feeling for stairs in a dark house and finding them. The dis-equilibrist working by elision, paraphrase, generic timing. Her concourse in the bar is with a bottle. She has exchanged identities with its glass walls. There is so much cognac inside her that she would like by inverse proportion to put part of herself inside the brandy bottle. Or is it Pernod? There's an alarming displace-ment of volume in both bottles. After the failure of her concerts at Olympia, she's singing in a small club to earn her airflight home. Somatically wasted, she's still dressed in a five hundred dollar gown. She can't see the audience. She concentrates on forgetting hearing herself sing. In her mind the past is evoked through the lyrics. Old lovers' faces, foggy days, the hope that love would this time be requited.

She comes back to herself and loses herself. There's the park again. She can remember flying above it. It was the colour of a crushed grape from the air. She wanted to point it out, but the dramatic increase in altitude had prevented her being sure it was a park, or that it really was there. Clouds had fluffed up her vision. But it was a moment of belief. There might be gold lions and gold bears in that park. And prophetic voices. Like a train heard in the night or the amplified premonition of a waterfall carried on the sound-waves like the irate motor of a bee trapped in a bottle. Departures have always been journeys, the descent into sleep, leaving the dressing-room to come on stage. The little vale-dictions which are initiatory preparations for death.

The park returns as an obsessive image. There aren't words for its inner reality. She sees it while she is singing. There's an iron gate at the end of one path, roses clambering all over it, and right in the distance a blaze of ionized light. She closes her eyes and there's a weightless hand on her wrist, like an energized bracelet. One step forward and she'll disappear for ever into the blue.

It's Not Because

Autumn, and black leaves roof the park. There's an hour Billie comes on in the heart. Everything's suspended for her confessional concession to pain. A marriage of the listener's inner dialogue with words not happening in time.

When Johnny Square goes home, he changes into a cocktail skirt. A draggy interlude in which he calls himself Scarlet. In that two hour space he can make himself up to look like Billie. All the photographs are there. Sometimes the lake walks right up to the house, and knocks on the window with a log. Scarlet's all right about it, she peels off leaves from the outside walls in the morning.

Scarlet has written out a list of Billie's ten favourite songs. Dizzy Gillespie's 'Round About Midnight', Ella Fitzgerald's 'Lady Be Good', Errol Garner's 'Cool Blues', Lester Young's 'Those Foolish Things', Gene Ammon's 'My Foolish Heart', Nat Cole's 'Jet', Woody Herman's 'Detour Ahead', Oscar Peterson's 'Tenderly', George Shearing's 'When Your Love Has Gone', and Louis Armstrong's 'You're Just in Love'. The pigment in her thinking was always blue.

Scarlet returns to being Johnny Square at 9 o'clock. He has a rendezvous with Gina Cube. Gina's all woman. Her sunglasses are backcombed into her gelled hair. She morphs the configurations in Johnny's mind. She knows he'd like to be the perfect woman. And when Billie's voice is there, they list the icons in their lives. The young Bardot pouting at the camera, and the one whose name they never can recall, glammed up and solitary, lying on a leopard skin towel under an Evian water-blue sky. Death is also a part of that mystery. A smoky aura. A black eye clicking on in the sky like a motion sensor.

At 11 o'clock Johnny is Scarlet again and Gina Johnny. They exchange clothes. Billie's still singing. But where is Billie? Is there a recording studio for the dead? A place built on another star? Johnny likes to think that Billie's repertoire is infinite. He'll get to hear it one day, but he'll never catch up with it all, not even by quantum leaps. Her psychic biography is still being written. If he listens, he can hear a microphone slammed down in deep space. The sonic reverb's like thunder.

CALLING NOWHERE

The time delay registers. There's a dream
in which she jumps in the Mississippi
and meets herself on the opposite bank
as someone else. When the film cuts
she's lost her memory. The zany hat,
six oranges, the bird-cage, red handbag
aren't hers, nor is the hotel room
identifiably her own. Her voice
has gone long distance. It's the other side
that's calling her, she must have left something
on the river bank in that dream
or cryptomnesiac reality,
and now her hand must cross a continent
in its retrieving arc. Is it a life
she left behind, swimming across that gap
by some motivating autonomy,
and is a life reclaimable? It beats
hard in its dying like a fish, bright scales
scattered along the jetty edge.
The woman she'd encountered wore her coat
and jewels, carried an album sleeve,
and scared her off by clapping her gloved hands.
She's in the wrong room. Someone's at her side,
the sheet drawn up to spilling hair,
and it's not somebody she knew last night,
and now she crawls out of bed, looks around
and knows there's nowhere in the world to hide.

FORGETTING

An orange ball bounces into real time,
an orange day. There's always an alert
to being who you are, instant recall
of data feedback, no blank gap
in consciousness, and memory
brilliant like autumn leaves frisking a lake.

How to forget experience
and not identify with broken love?
Old lovers waiting at a train station,
they haven't changed, swim into view,
they're headed for the last stop on the line,
the gold gates open to a park
in which they'll disappear
and reappear in other lives
with other loves in April rain. And shine.

Forgetting means going away
to a square in a foreign town,
a precinct with nobody there
or white shadows against white walls,
no anything.
                    It means staying asleep
all afternoon, the crowded day outside,
rain falling over water in a dream
that's out of time and somewhere deep.

OH NO NO NO OH LADY DAY
Lou Reed

Lou's vicious monotone, post-Lady Day,
lifting her looks as iconography
to a later decade, chasing her need
all over town inside a song
spitting anger like pomegranate seeds,
demanding like we do that fame
reaches the dead, blows through their consciousness
like synergized starlight, illuminates

the big injustices, the ones heard far too late
like Rimbaud, Nerval, Baudelaire,
like Nietzsche, Blake and Billie Holiday
and all the others staring out
of a black window in the sky

at interplanetary lights.
The song beats words across the street
in its dispassionate acclaim
for Billie and her ruined cast

singled for posthumous address.
Live, it electrifies from wall to wall
as though the singer lit her way,
turned institutions upside down
and stared out at white light flooding the hall.

BLUE LOU

I know that title somewhere, it's a song
circa 1930, the jazzation
afforded a voice bluesy as a horn.
Today, the title's onomatopoeia
brings to my mind the modern skies we've known
counting decades since Ashbery
jump-started a new poetry.
Blues as a jeans shade, and an abstract tone
seen like the future through a smoked window.

Day in day out I try to read
a meaning on the other side of light.
Your letter came the sooner for my need,
opening it had your voice jump in the room.

Sometimes my solitude's like depth
I'll never measure with my hand.
A place down there. The waters break
if the diver jumps flat.

I wait for you to telephone
a year away, a future call
from time I've never reached. You'll tell me how
the changes have occurred, and what I'll find
when I arrive, your house is painted white,
it's blue today with creeper on one wall.

Cut Up In The Doldrums

Cordoned off with black curtains	hours at sea
crossing the dateline orange slingbacks	blue hours at
sea I've gone from wearing dresses	sea-blue hours
to being a 14-year-old girl	hours at sea
the Panama Hotel the Gulf	green hours at
sea at three I led my mother across the street	sea-green hours
not the other way round accompaniment	hours at sea
a sloth-induced dance shifting weight	grey hours at
sea obsession with ironing	sea-grey hours
usually sex and drugs oxymoronic	hours at sea
a girl wants diamonds shoegazing	white hours at
sea the preserve of the brain dead	sea-white hours
jumping ship into torch generic flame	hours at sea
apparently permanently stoned	pink hours at
sea beyond the fringe set of black clothes	sea-pink hours
circular breathing zeitgeist surfers	hours at sea
string without the dog	mauve hours at
sea I've opened at the Famous Door	sea-mauve hours
a four-bar introduction	hours at sea
America's No. 1 Song Stylist	red hours at
sea most of the show reverse time	sea-red hours
twitching my ten silk toes at Ecuador	hours at sea
the Turkish hostage cracks his sunglasses	orange hours at
sea a tyre exploding in Berlin	sea-orange hours
calm in the satin avenues	hours at sea
blue hours at sea sea-blue hours and	blue hours at
sea nosing for ever blue through	sea-blue hours

I Cover the Waterfront

Lost by the docks in a blue Burberry,
she lights a cigarette, and collar up
glances at the sea's pooled opacity,

its sleekly oilskinned surface, black on black,
the tangy air smelling of iodine, rust.
She's quit her taxi, and her quirky tack

brings her the singer, face up to her song.
An even four keeps rhythm in her head,
the syncopation pushing her along

to smooth rather than crease the lyric line.
Most ships are lit up. Practical imageries
slide on water, dazzle, and take a shine.

Nothing like harbours for isolation,
her busted marriages swim in her head.
A port's lonelier than a train station

and tears raindrop the break in a left cheek.
Her love, her man, there's nothing more to say.
Singing's for those who can no longer speak.

Tomorrow's still possible, will it bring
the perfect stranger with gold on his tongue,
a moated château buried in his ring,

the bedroom window concealed by ivy?
She walks away, directing her own film.
A late night bar attracts her on the quay.

TORCH

Hitting that second interval down deep
before the smoky bottom note, it's stairs
collapsing in the dark, a voice

proclaiming travel through the years,
childhood abandoned in a breezy dress
beside a looping river, and the star
buried inside a blue Lincoln
broken down on a fast highway
somewhere in mid-continent.

So the transition in her register
to tragic intonation, arms held out
to unrequited love, she lifts a hand
direct out of the memory
as though crossing a bridge from night to day
the fog burning off in a pink halo.

Listening to Herself

In a black boa and a black silk slip. She feeds on the digital impulses, the restrained adoption of melismata to embellish shorter phrase lengths. Solitary days at 26 West 87th Street, near Central Park. Every month there's a blue envelope on her mat containing a thousand dollars, from an anonymous donor. The money not only keeps her alive, but it's a reminder that her voice is an immutable entity which will always go on living. Icons live by transferable image and mood associations in others, so they are not subject to being fixed in time. Someone's looking at a photo of her as she was in 1944, and it's 1958. He associates the photograph with the voice, and so she will never grow old. It's like walking through a wind-tunnel to find on emergence your body clock has been put back 30 years. The reversal instates a sense of being displaced in missing time. When she goes out shopping, lonely on the Avenues, she embodies the multiple images which comprise her legendized identity. Someone's seeing her in 1940, and someone in 2025. It's all the same. It's a parapsychological configuration of immortality. She can retrieve her youth by buying her own records. She can deepen the experience by listening to them.

And there's the geologist from Czechoslovakia, who calls at the apartment. Alice. Alice is always there. She polishes Billie's neurons and memories. They each sit in dark glasses in different corners of the room. Billie doesn't like any music but her own. She reviews her phrasing with a commitment to awareness, and with the concentrated excitement of an aficionado. In that way she's always on. Trapezoids and rhombs of late afternoon light chink through the blinds in a paraphrasable entry. Listening to herself is the in thing at 25 West 87th Street. The traffic has the sussuration of wild surf. Billie's hedonistic mania, which was always a substitute for profound introspection, has slowed to a phased autumnal glow. But listening to herself involves immediate travel on a trajectory through so many terminals. All the way back to where? A visual snatch at eyes seen in an audience once, or turnips spilling out of the tailboard of a red lorry crashed on the road? It could be anywhere. She kicks her shoes off. Her voice is talking to her through the speakers. The trees outside are shedding antlers in the park.

FAME THAT'S TAINTED, FAME THAT'S BLUE

And in a day a week a month a year the work progresses and comes back on itself. Being a cult means inciting the envy and recriminative hostility of the mainstream. Billie's offstage language doesn't suit society. She 'motherfucks' her way to neologistic elisions. A drug argot. A language that's like untutored poetry. Genet had it, but with literary sophistication.

So she travels down one arm of America, and up the other. It's the same sort of intensely admirative audience in every club. But it gets her nowhere. Back for the tenth time on an unbreakable loop. There are macroscopic black holes in the unconscious. Most of her biological information disappears into those energy fields. And there is always interruption. A backdrop of voices intruding on her focused concentration. It cuts into her like schizophrenic interference. All of that muzzy inconsequential chatter. And every time for her is as important as the first time. She has to hear herself to know if she can still make it.

> 'Lady Day without the gutsy glamour of her most intimate appearances in dark-filled clubs, stretched elegance far in white regalia . . . her particular type of vitality in her famous "Billie's Blues" was ill-placed.'

She emanates a torchy halo. The audience will never care enough about the tiny particulars she creates for herself. And selling out would mean severing that chord attached to anxiety and menace. If she repatriated to safety she'd lose her way. She would unwrite herself and be simply another performer. Singing instead of crying on the word.

She lives in a continuity of inner space. What time is it out there, and does it really matter? If she gives up the outer clock, then she can live permanently in her own reality. One show to another, the gaps in between filled by white sleep. White plateaux on which to remember nothing. Not even the white windmill waving its arm for attention. And where anyhow did the wind come from in a dream? The right side or the left side, north or south? She's lost the higher earnings, the national attention she could have achieved. She's resigned to inveterate belief in herself and mistrust in others. She sees herself wearing a white dress on a white plateau. She's going away somewhere. But there's always the hope that the transformation will happen. The break which redresses all earlier injustices. There's so much gold light in the stars. Her car's driving that way.